A Charlie Brown Christmas™

ISBN 978-1-4234-5648-3

Visit Peanuts© on the Internet at
www.snoopy.com

HAL•LEONARD®
CORPORATION

7777 W. BLUEMOUND RD. P.O. BOX 13819 MILWAUKEE, WI 53213

Visit Hal Leonard Online at
www.halleonard.com

CHRISTMAS IS COMING

By VINCE GUARALDI

Rock Bossa Nova

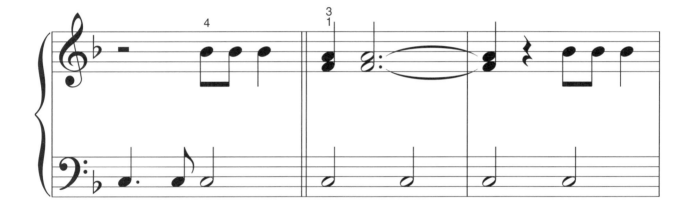

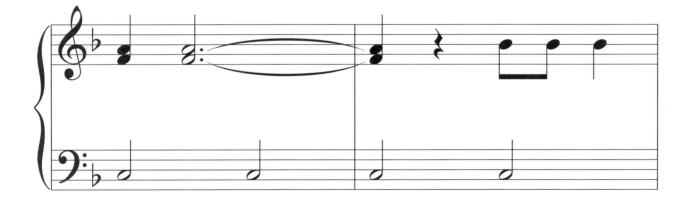

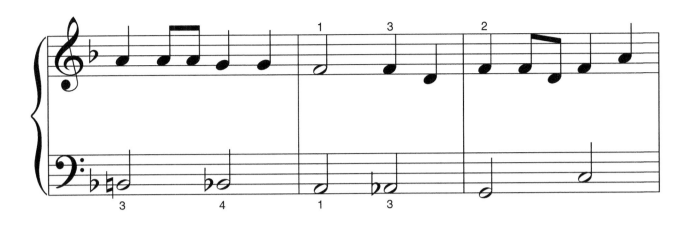

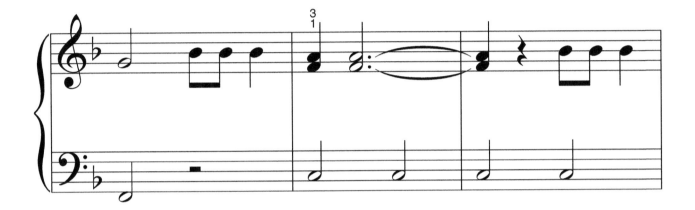

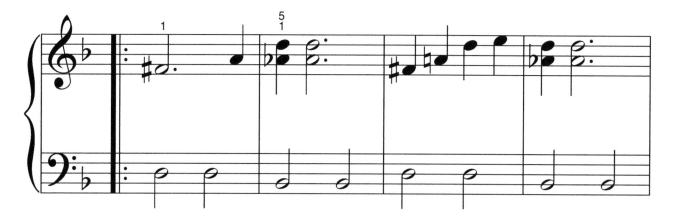

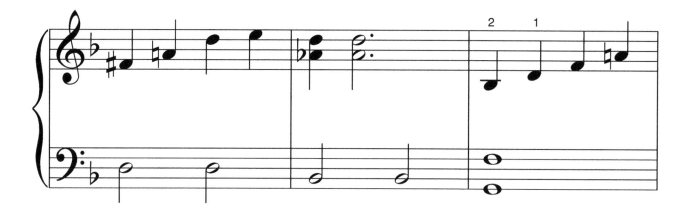

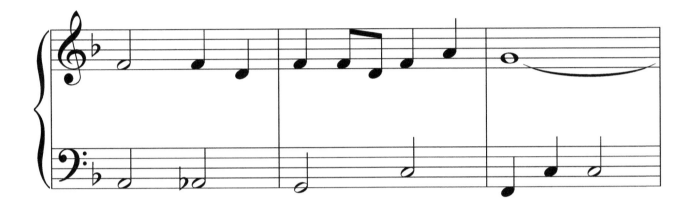

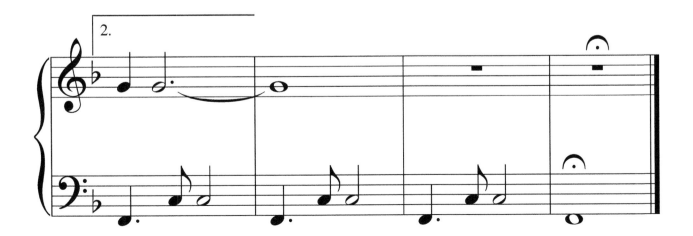

THE CHRISTMAS SONG
(Chestnuts Roasting on an Open Fire)

Music and Lyric by MEL TORME
and ROBERT WELLS

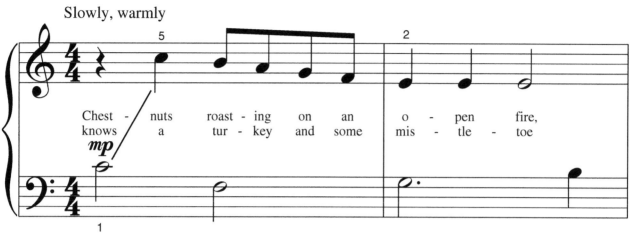

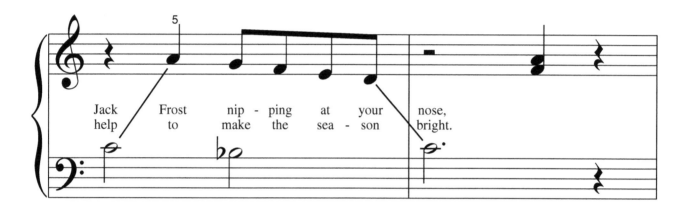

find it hard to sleep to - night. _____ They know that

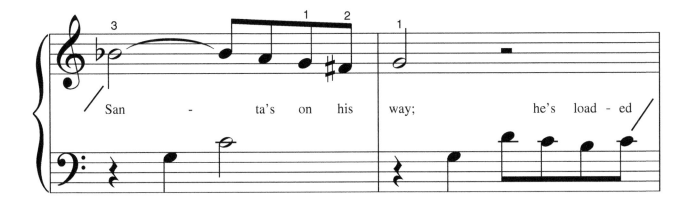

San - ta's on his way; he's load - ed

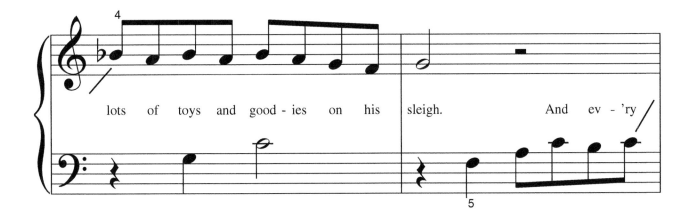

lots of toys and good - ies on his sleigh. And ev - 'ry

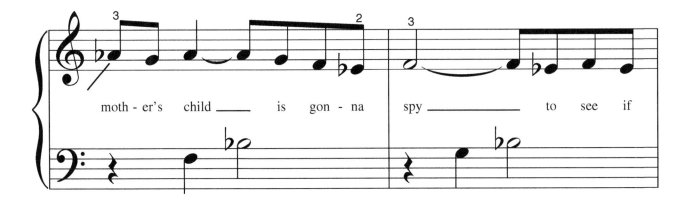

moth - er's child _____ is gon - na spy _____ to see if

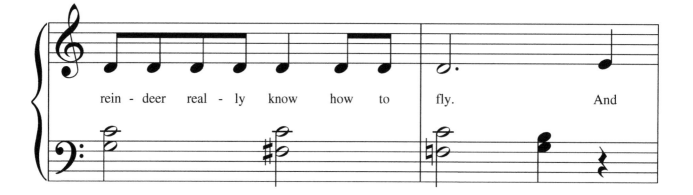

rein - deer real - ly know how to fly. And

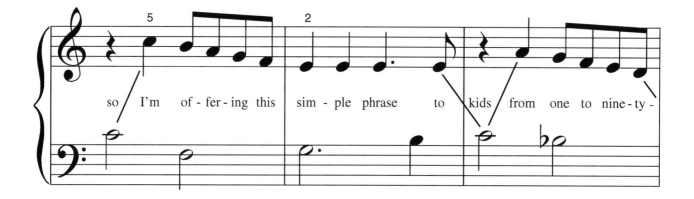

so I'm of - fer - ing this sim - ple phrase to kids from one to nine - ty -

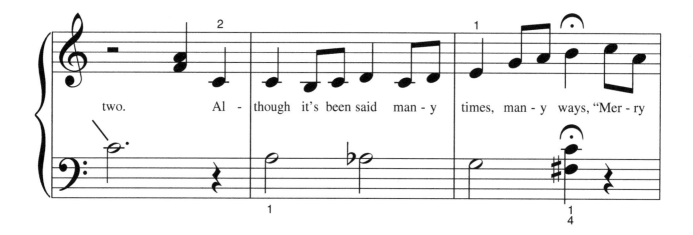

two. Al - though it's been said man - y times, man - y ways, "Mer - ry

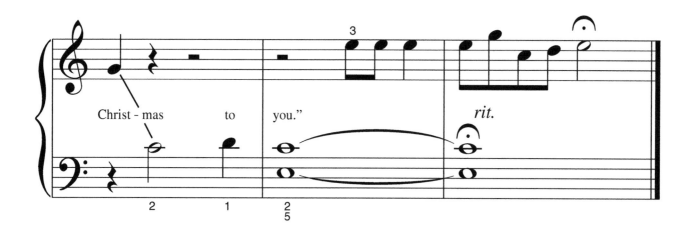

Christ - mas to you." *rit.*

CHRISTMAS TIME IS HERE

Words by LEE MENDELSON
Music by VINCE GUARALDI

Christ - mas time is here,
Snow - flakes in the air,

hap - pi - ness and cheer,
car - ols ev - 'ry - where.

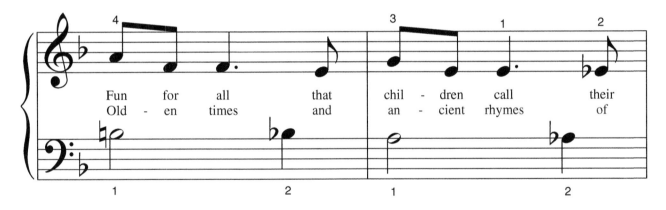

Fun for all that chil - dren call their
Old - en times and an - cient rhymes of

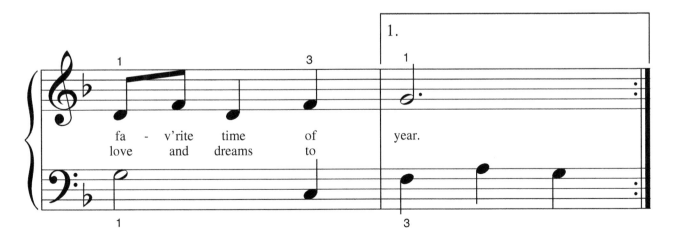

1.
fa - v'rite time of year.
love and dreams to

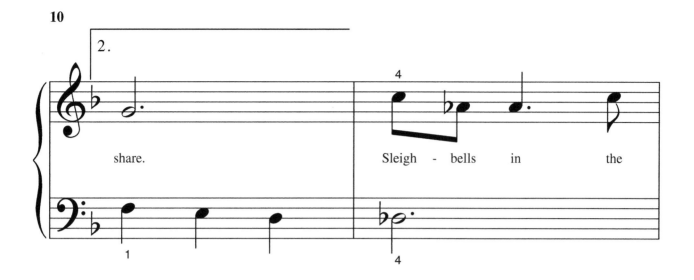

share.　Sleigh - bells in the

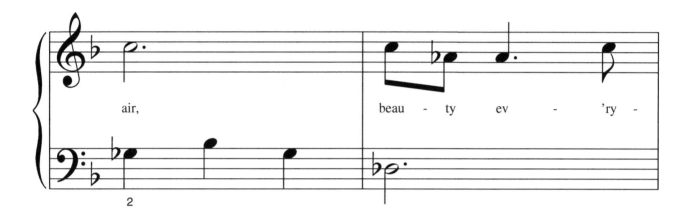

air,　beau - ty ev - 'ry -

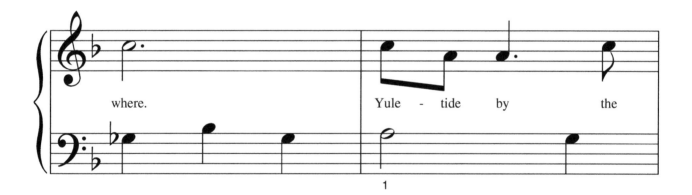

where.　Yule - tide by the

fire - side and joy - ful mem - 'ries

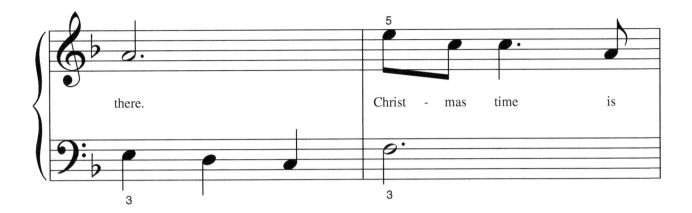

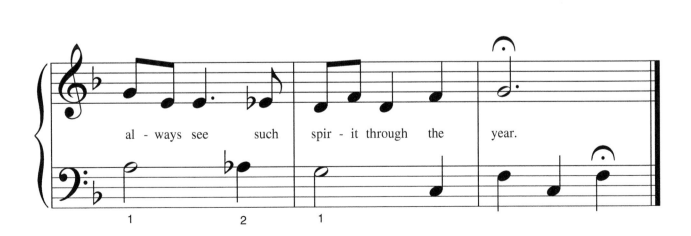

FÜR ELISE

By LUDWIG VAN BEETHOVEN
Arranged by VINCE GUARALDI

Flowing

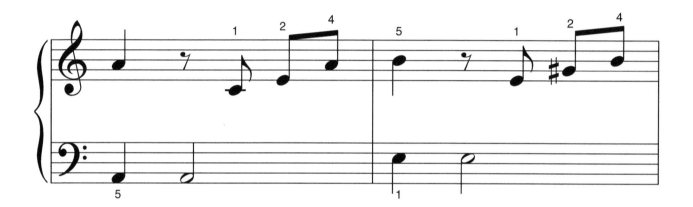

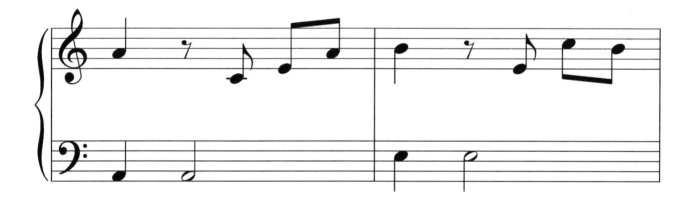

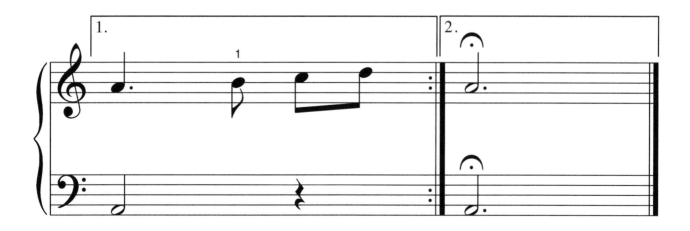

LINUS AND LUCY

By VINCE GUARALDI

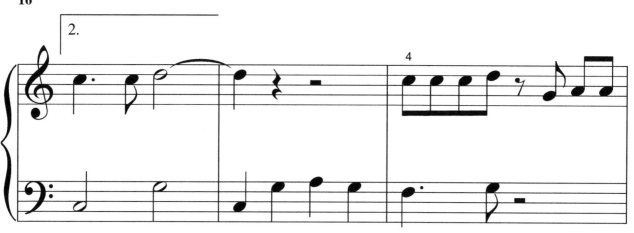

HARK, THE HERALD ANGELS SING

Traditional
Arranged by VINCE GUARALDI

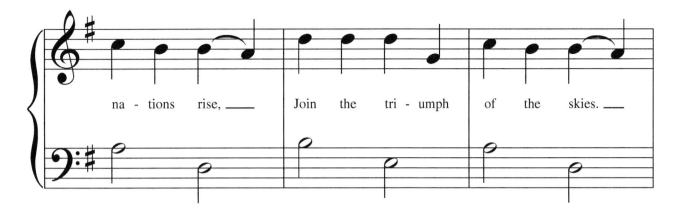

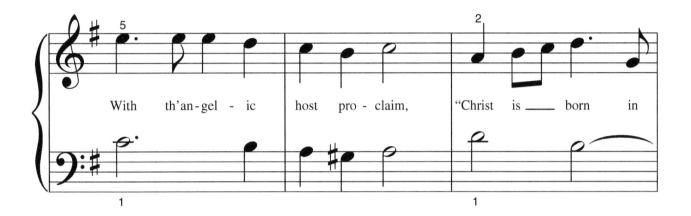

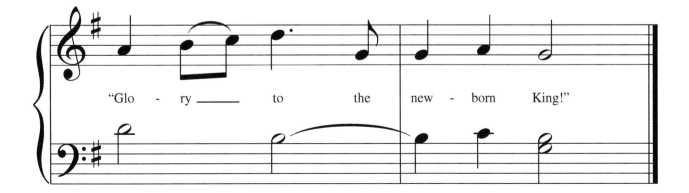

MY LITTLE DRUM

By VINCE GUARALDI

Moderately

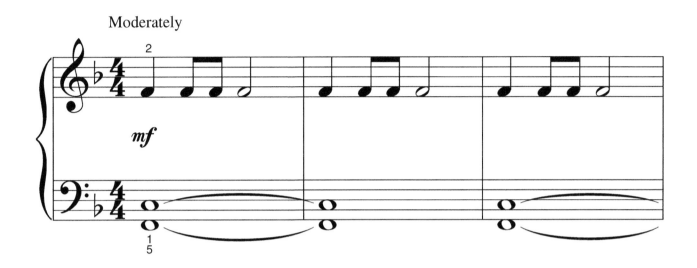

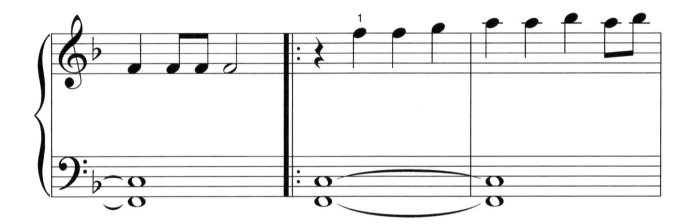

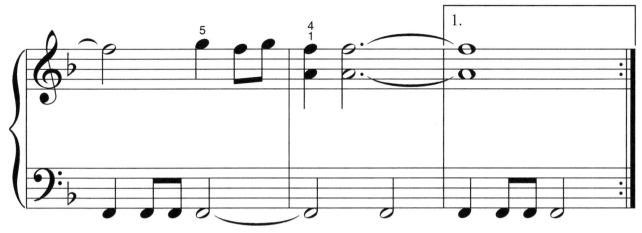

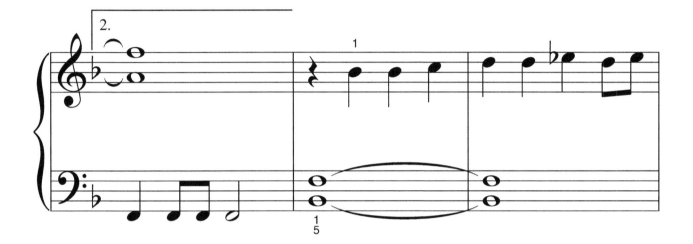

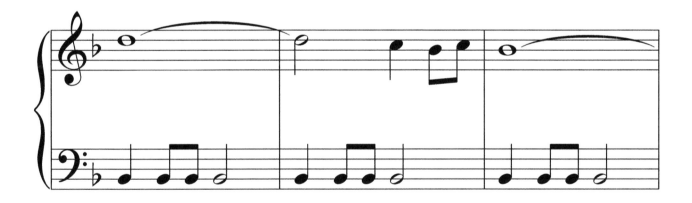

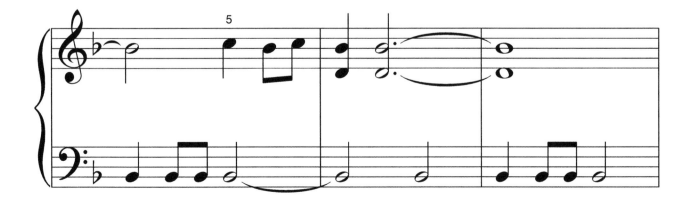

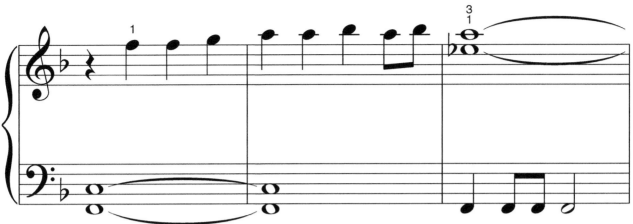

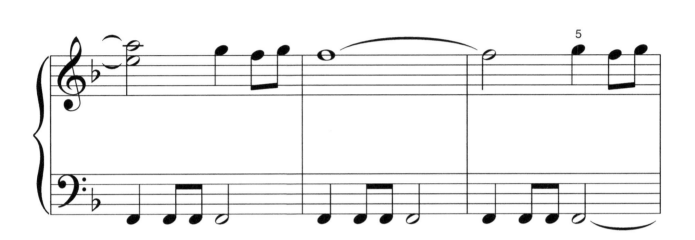

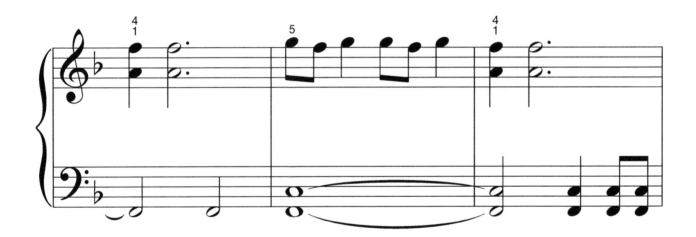

rit.

SKATING

By VINCE GUARALDI

Bright Jazz Waltz

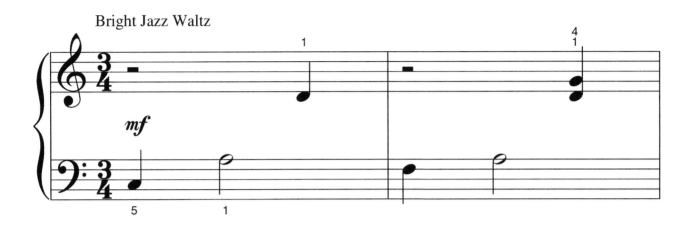

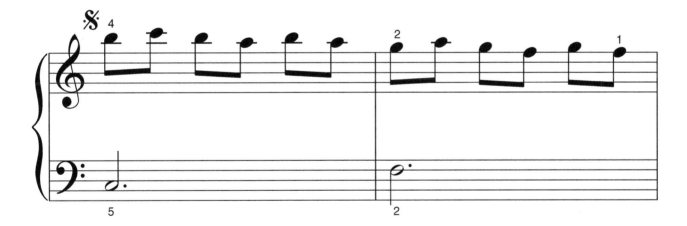

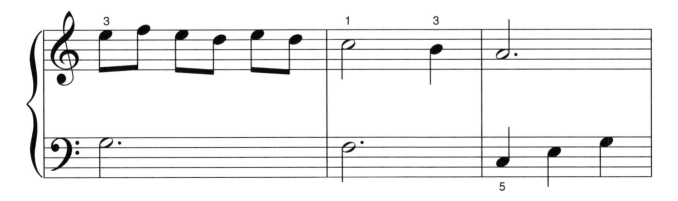

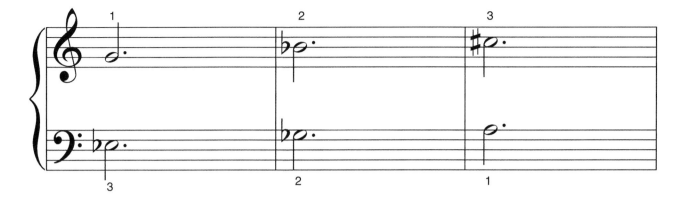

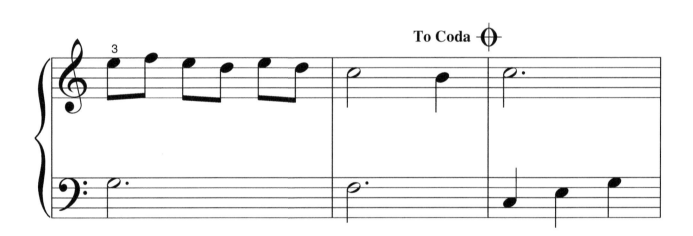

To Coda ⊕

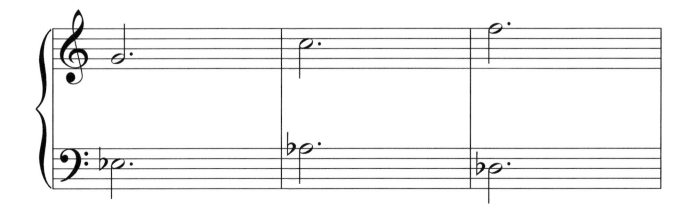

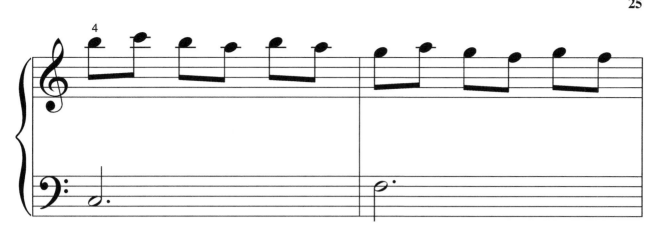

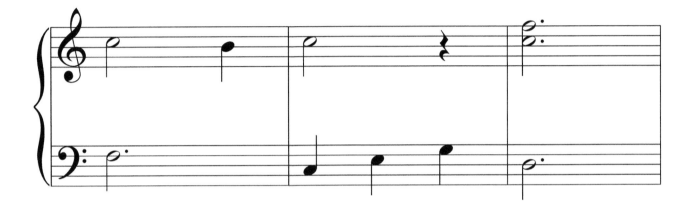

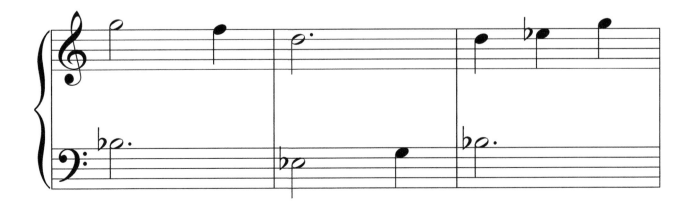

CODA

D.S. al Coda

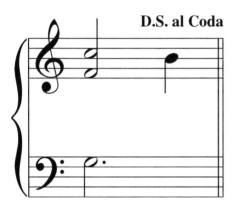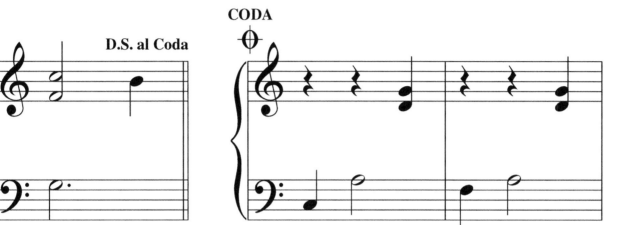

rit.

O TANNENBAUM

Traditional
Arranged by Vince Guaraldi

Moderately

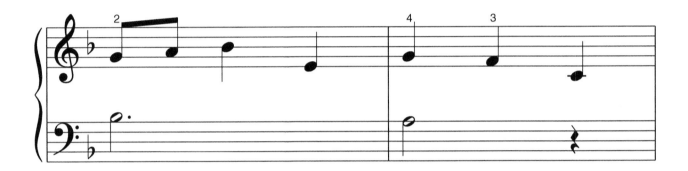

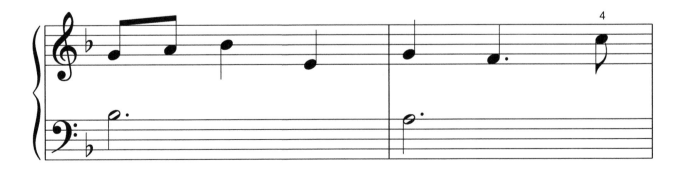

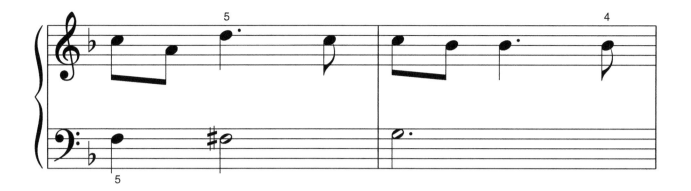

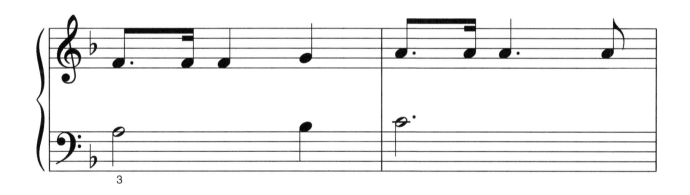

WHAT CHILD IS THIS

Traditional
Arranged by Vince Guaraldi

Slowly

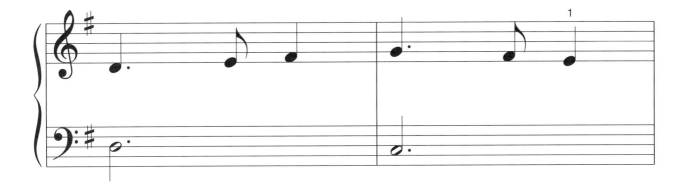

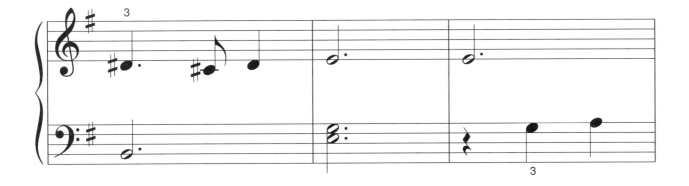

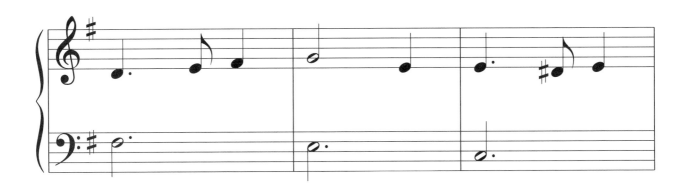

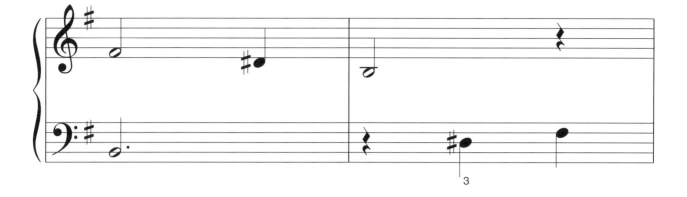

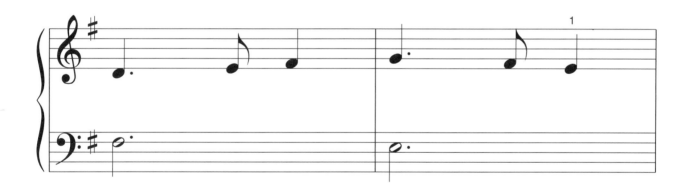

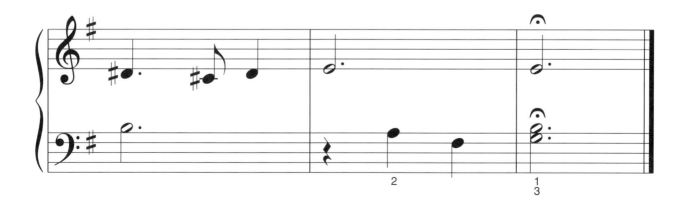